On or Under

Where's Eddie?

T0045151

Daniel Nunn

Illustrations by Steve Walker

Hide and Seek

Raintree

Chicago, Illinois

www.capstonepub.com
Visit our website to find out more information about Heinemann-Raintree books.

To order:
Phone 800-747-4992
Visit www.capstonepub.com to browse our catalog and order online.

© 2013 Raintree is an imprint of Capstone Global Library, LLC
Chicago, Illinois

All rights reserved. No part of this publication may be reproduced or transmitted in any form or by any means, electronic or mechanical, including photocopying, recording, taping, or any information storage and retrieval system, without permission in writing from the publisher.

Edited by Dan Nunn, Rebecca Rissman, and Sian Smith
Designed by Joanna Hinton-Malivoire
Picture research by Mica Brancic
Originated by Capstone Global Library. Ltd.
Production by Victoria Fitzgerald
Printed and bound in United States
012320 003162
16 15 14 13 12
10 9 8 7 6 5 4 3 2 1

Library of Congress Cataloging-in-Publication Data
Nunn, Daniel.
On or under : where's Eddie? / Daniel Nunn.
p. cm.—(Hide and seek)
ISBN 978-1-4109-4711-6 (hb)—ISBN 978-1-4109-4717-8 (pb) 1. English language—Prepositions—Juvenile literature. I. Title.
PE1335.N86 2013
428.2—dc23 2012003789

Acknowledgments
We would like to thank the following for permission to reproduce photographs: Shutterstock pp.5 (© Ingrid Prats), 6 (© NeonLight), 7 (© Andrii Ospishchev), 8 (© Adisa), 9 (© Alexander Chaikin), 10 (© Ihnatovich Maryia), 11, 12 (© Worachat Sodsri), 13, 14 (© Ronald Sumners), 15, 16 (© Kirill Vorobyev), 17, 18 (© Chin Kit Sen), 19, 20 (© iadams), 21 (© Breadmaker), 22 (© Alexia Khruscheva), 23 (© Dmitry Rukhlenko).

Front cover photograph of a tractor reproduced with permission of Shutterstock (© NanoStock).

Every effort has been made to contact copyright holders of any material reproduced in this book. Any omissions will be rectified in subsequent printings if notice is given to the publisher.

Contents

Meet Eddie the Elephant 4

On 6

Under 8

Find Eddie! 10

True or False? 21

Answers and More! 24

Be careful when you hide!
Eddie can hide in places where people can't. Hiding inside things can be very dangerous. Always ask an adult if it is safe first.

Meet Eddie the Elephant

This is Eddie the Elephant.

Eddie loves to play hide and seek!

On

Sometimes Eddie hides **on** things.

On means on top of something.

Under
Sometimes Eddie hides **under** things.

Under means below something.

Find Eddie!

Can you find Eddie?
Count to 10, then off you go!

Where is Eddie?
Is he **on** the table or **under** the table?

Eddie is **on** the table.

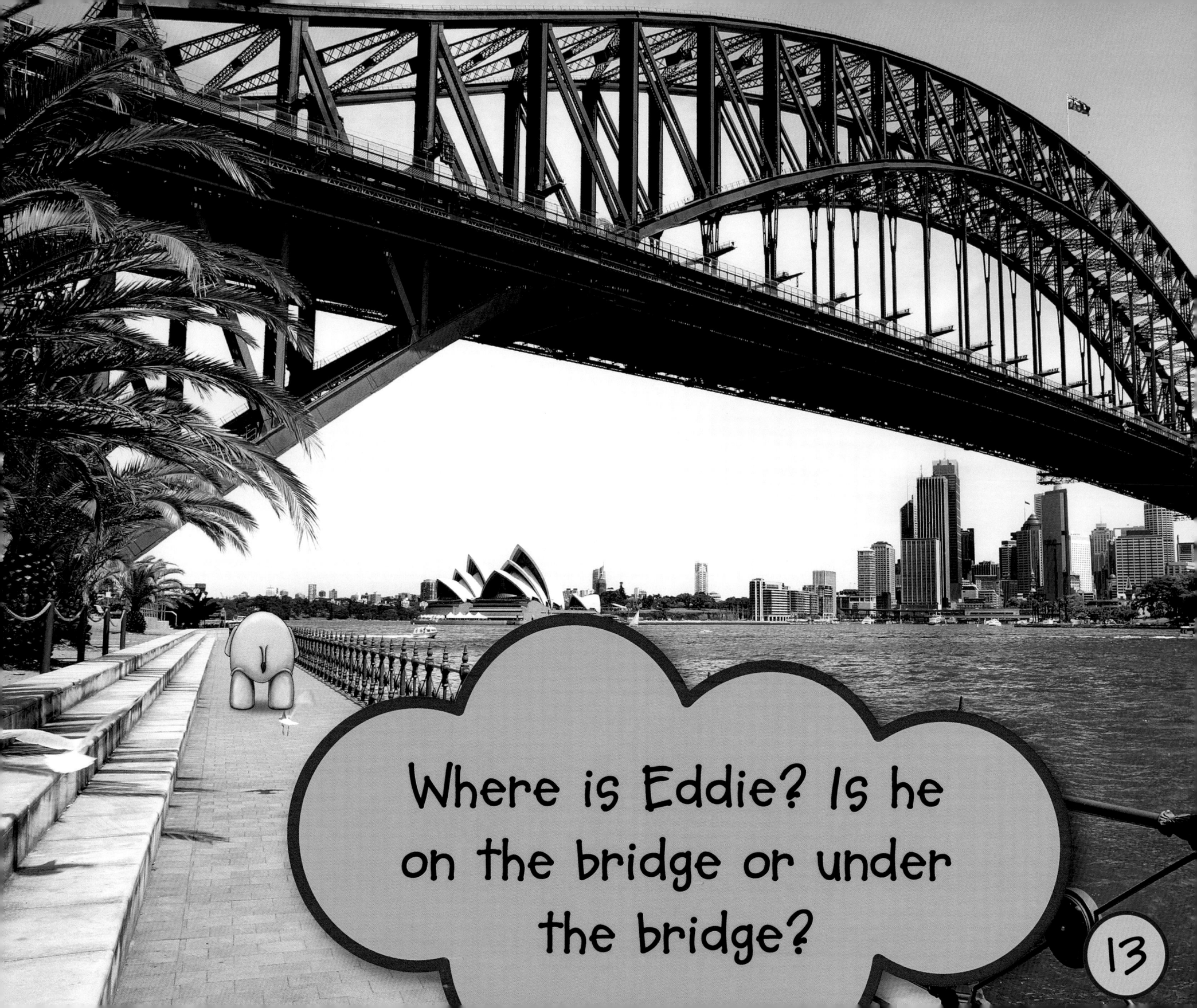
Where is Eddie? Is he on the bridge or under the bridge?

Eddie is **under** the bridge.

Where is Eddie?
Is he **on** the cat or **under** the cat?

Eddie is **on** the cat.

Where is Eddie? Is he **on** the yellow pillow or **under** the yellow pillow?

Eddie is **under** the yellow pillow.

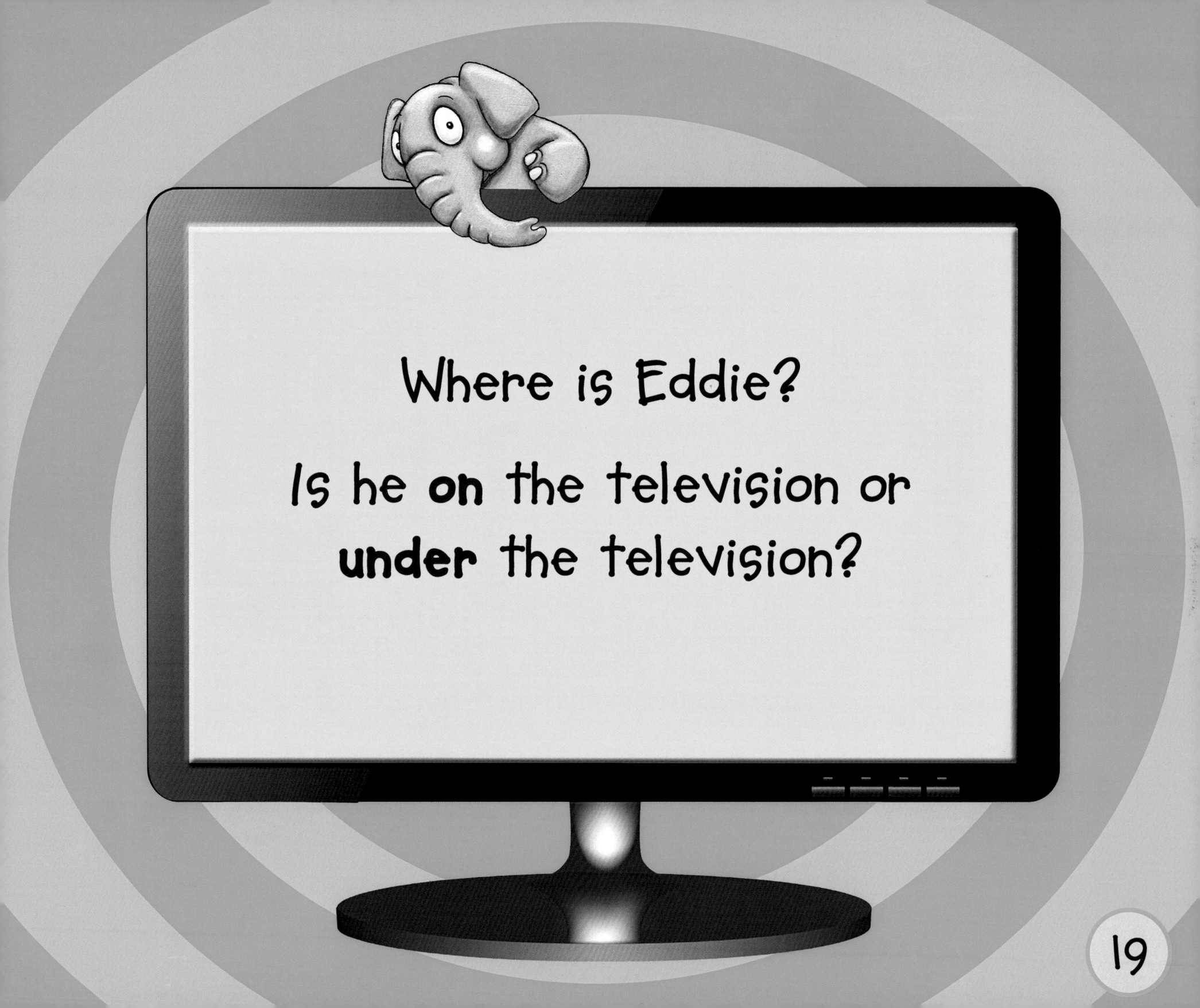

Where is Eddie?

Is he **on** the television or **under** the television?

Eddie is **on** the television.

True or False?

1. Eddie is **under** the bed. True or false?

You can find the answers on page 24.

2. Eddie is **under** the horse.
True or false?

3. Eddie is **under** the hat.
True or false?

Answers and More!

True or false?

1. True! Eddie is **under** the bed.
2. False! Eddie is **on** the horse.
3. True! Eddie is **under** the hat.

Where can Eddie hide next?

Look around the room you are in.

What could Eddie hide **on**?

What could Eddie hide **under**?